The Last Stand

The Final Military Campaign of General George Armstrong Custer

Jennifer Silate

rosen central

Primary Source™

The Rosen Publishing Group, Inc., New York

Published in 2004 by The Rosen Publishing Group, Inc.
29 East 21st Street, New York, NY 10010

Editor: Scott Waldman
Book Design: Michael DeLisio
Photo Researcher: Rebecca Anguin-Cohen
Series Photo Researcher: Jeff Wendt
Photo Credits: Cover (left), title page, p. 18 © SuperStock, Inc.; cover (right) illustration © Debra Wainwright/The Rosen Publishing Group; pp. 6, 29 Still Picture Branch, National Archives and Records Administration; pp. 10, 14 Western History Collections, University of Oklahoma Libraries; p. 22 Courtesy of the South Dakota State Historical Society-State Archives; p. 30 United States Military Academy; p. 31 Southwest Museum; p. 32 Denver Public Library, Western History Collection, Joseph Kossuth Dixon, X-31275.

First Edition

Library of Congress Cataloging-in-Publication Data

Silate, Jennifer.
  The last stand : the final military campaign of General George
  Armstrong Custer / by Jennifer Silate.—1st ed.
  p. cm.—(Great moments in American history)
  Summary: Describes the causes, events, and aftermath of the battle in
  1876 between soldiers of the United States army, commanded by General
  George Armstrong Custer, and Indian warriors of the Cheyenne and Sioux
  nations.
  ISBN 0-8239-4353-4 (lib. bdg.)
  1. Little Bighorn, Battle of the, Mont., 1876—Juvenile literature.
  2. Custer, George Armstrong, 1839-1876—Juvenile literature. [1. Little
  Bighorn, Battle of the, Mont., 1876. 2. Custer, George Armstrong,
  1839-1876.] I. Title. II. Series.

E83.876.S53 2004
973.8'2—dc21

                                  2003009733

Manufactured in the United States of America

CONTENTS

Preface

George Armstrong Custer's career in the U.S. military began poorly. In 1861, he graduated last in his class at West Point, a school that trains army officers. However, after West Point, Custer fought in the American Civil War. During the Civil War, Custer became well known for the fearless way he fought in battle. When he was twenty-three years old, Custer was made a general. He was the youngest general in the U.S. Army.

After the Civil War ended in 1865, Custer continued to serve in the military. The following year, Custer was sent into the land west of the Mississippi River. He and his men worked to keep settlers safe from attacks by Native Americans. Native Americans in the area did not want the settlers to take over their land. Fighting broke out between the Native Americans and settlers.

When the settlers started mining for gold in the Black Hills of South Dakota, the fighting worsened. The Black Hills were a holy place for Native Americans. The U.S. government also planned on building a railroad through land that had been promised to some Native American tribes. The idea of a railroad on their lands angered many Native Americans.

In 1875, President Ulysses S. Grant ordered many Native Americans to live on reservations. On May 17, 1876, Custer and his men left Fort Lincoln in what is now North Dakota. They were on their way to fight with Native Americans who would not move onto a reservation. What Custer did not know was that it would be the last stand he would ever make on a battlefield.

In most photos of George Armstrong Custer, he appears rugged, with long hair. This photo, however, shows him as an older military leader. It was taken in 1876, the year he died.

Chapter One

ON THE MOVE

*I*t was June 21, 1876. The sun was hot on General George Armstrong Custer's face. He and his men had been marching for days. They had finally arrived at the mouth of Rosebud Creek in North Dakota. Custer had traveled there to meet with his commanders, General Alfred Terry, General George Crook, and Colonel John Gibbon. The men were meeting to decide how they were going to attack a group of Sioux Indians who would not move onto a reservation.

"Good afternoon, Custer," Terry said as he shook Custer's hand. "We have been waiting for you to arrive."

"Good afternoon, General," Custer replied. "Will we be meeting this evening?"

"Yes, we are meeting on the *Far West* steamship at six o'clock. We have a lot to discuss, Custer.

Yesterday, Indian tracks were found not far from here. I think we may get them this time," Terry said.

"That's good to hear, General. Thank you," Custer said as he turned to leave. Custer was looking forward to the meeting. He hoped that he would do well in the coming battle between his men and the Native Americans. A success would help his career. He was sure the army would win.

That night, Custer met with the other commanders on the *Far West*.

"Good evening, gentlemen," Terry began. "As you know, we have found some fresh Indian tracks near Rosebud Creek. I believe that the Sioux Indians have left the tracks on their way to the Little Bighorn Valley. Custer, I want you to follow the Indians up the Rosebud and into Little Bighorn. You will make the first attack. Six Indian scouts working for us will go with you. They know the area well and will be a great help. You already have the most men, but I will give you four more companies to make sure that you are not outnumbered."

"I do not think the extra men will be necessary," Custer said boldly. "My men can handle anything that comes our way. The scouts will get us to the battle and we will win."

"Well, at least take a Gatling gun. It can fire as many bullets as forty men," Terry suggested.

"General, the Gatling gun is so heavy that we would not be able to follow the Indians quickly enough. We will lose them," Custer replied. "Trust me, my men can win this battle."

"All right, Custer. I hope you're right. The other commanders and I will surround Little Bighorn. Your attack will push the Indians north and we will be there waiting for them," Terry said.

"When should we set off?" Custer asked.

"You and your men should leave as soon as possible," Terry replied. "Good luck on your missions and I hope to see you all again soon."

As he left the steamship, Custer whistled his favorite song. He was excited about the coming battle and was sure that it would be another success for his career.

The Sioux did not stay in one place for long. They needed to follow herds of animals, like buffalo, for food. This 1891 photo of a Sioux camp in South Dakota shows what their settlements looked like.

Chapter Two

NEWS FROM THE SCOUTS

Custer and his men left Rosebud Creek the next afternoon. They marched for two days. They passed several places where Native Americans had camped. On the evening of June 24, Custer's scout, Bloody Knife, brought some news.

"Sir, I think we are catching up with the Sioux," Bloody Knife said. "The tracks are not even two days old. The Sioux may be only thirty miles away in the Little Bighorn Valley. But there's something else. There are many more tracks than there were before. More Indians have joined the Sioux," Bloody Knife said.

"Lieutenant Varnum!" Custer shouted when Bloody Knife had finished speaking. Lieutenant Varnum hurried to join Custer.

"Yes, General Custer," he said.

"Lieutenant, our scouts believe the Indians are in

the valley. Take some scouts to the lookout that the Indians use to view Little Bighorn. I will lead the men to the opening between the Little Bighorn River and Rosebud Creek. Report back to me with what you find," Custer said.

Custer and his men marched until about 3:00 A.M. the next morning when they finally stopped to rest. They had hardly stopped marching for 24 hours. Custer was in his tent, thinking about the coming battle when a messenger brought a note from Varnum.

General Custer:

The scouts have told me that they saw campfire smoke and ponies in the valley from an Indian village. They say the village is 3 miles long and only about 15 miles away. I could not see this with my own eyes, but I have no reason to doubt the truth of their report.

Your humble servant,

Lieutenant Charles A. Varnum

Custer believed the scouts had seen the Indian village. He planned to attack the village at the break of dawn on the following day, June 26.

Moments later, Custer's brother Thomas entered the tent. He was working with Custer.

"Did the scouts see anything?" Thomas asked.

"Yes. They say there is a large village in the valley," Custer replied.

"I have some bad news. A few of the men have seen Indians," Thomas said.

"Did the Indians see our men?" Custer asked.

"Yes, and the men said the Indians had supplies that had fallen from our mules. They must know we are here," Thomas said.

Custer knew that the Native Americans would run away from the soldiers if they thought the soldiers were coming. If the Native Americans ran, Custer would be responsible for their escape. On the other hand, his men were tired and Custer did not know how many Sioux were in the valley. Gibbon and Terry would not yet be anywhere near the valley. Custer decided to attack immediately. It was a decision he would soon regret.

Many people blamed Marcus A. Reno for the army's losses at the Battle of Little Bighorn. They claimed he was a coward. The courts found this to be untrue, but these attacks hurt Major Reno's career.

Chapter Three

RENO RETREATS

T he air was hot and still. The men had marched for several miles. Custer wiped dirt and sweat from his face. He had split up his men into several groups. He sent one group ahead, led by Captain Frederick Benteen, to look for signs of Sioux. The rest marched with Custer toward Little Bighorn. "Lieutenant Cooke!" Custer shouted to one of his officers.

"Yes, sir," Cooke said as he steered his horse toward Custer.

"Tell Major Reno to take his men to the south of the valley as quickly as he can. Tell him to attack the Sioux when he finds them. I will lead a group of soldiers to help him fight," Custer said.

After Major Reno received his orders, he immediately set off with the 175 men under his command to fight the Sioux. Once the men crossed the

15

Little Bighorn River, they saw the village. Reno's heart pounded in his chest. The village was much larger than he had expected. Still, he would follow his orders no matter how dangerous they were.

"All right men!" Reno shouted. "Charge!"

The men rode toward the village. The people there could see the great clouds of dust that were being made by the advancing soldiers. Screams filled the air. Women and children ran to take cover. The men jumped on their horses and grabbed guns and any other weapons they could find. Reno had surprised them, but the Native Americans were ready to fight.

Large numbers of Native American warriors rode toward Reno and his men. Reno was outnumbered. His soldiers could not fight back against so many warriors. He ordered his men to form a line behind some trees near the village.

Reno could see no sign of Custer and his men. *When are they going to get here?* he thought. Everywhere he looked, he saw his men being

killed by the enemy. Reno knew he could not win this fight without Custer's help. "Retreat!" he yelled. Reno and his soldiers rode as fast as they could back across the Little Bighorn River. They went to the top of a hill where it was easier for them to fight back against the Native Americans.

By this time, Captain Benteen and his men had also reached the village. They saw Reno and his men riding away. Benteen rode to meet Reno at the top of the hill. "We've lost at least thirty men, Captain!" Reno shouted to Benteen over the gunfire.

"I received orders to come to the village with supplies," Benteen said. "Have you seen Custer?"

"No, we're all alone out here," Reno replied.

"We'll stay here and fight," Benteen said. "Together we can take them."

Benteen and Reno didn't know it, but Custer and his men were about to begin their own battle at the north end of the village. And without their help, Custer would be in trouble.

By 1896 the Battle of Little Bighorn had become so famous that a large beer-maker issued this poster, *Custer's Last Fight*, for barrooms to display.

Chapter Four

THE BATTLE OF LITTLE BIGHORN

T he sun shone brightly over the valley. Custer looked down over the village. There were many more Native Americans than he had expected. Tepees stretched for miles along the valley. Dust and smoke rose into the cloudless sky a few miles down the river. Custer guessed that the dust and smoke he saw was from Reno's attack. What he did not know was that Reno had been forced to retreat.

Custer and his men marched toward the Little Bighorn River. As they got closer, they heard the chilling whoops of Native American war cries. Warriors on horseback were crossing the river and coming toward them. Custer's men were on a long hill above the river. Bullets whizzed past the soldiers as they struggled to fire their guns at the advancing warriors.

"We're being attacked, men!" Custer shouted. "Don't let them take the hill!"

The soldiers got off their horses and lined up at the edge of the hill. They fired at the warriors and stopped many from coming up the hill from the south. For a short while, the soldiers held back the warriors. However, their success would not last. Through the haze, Custer could see more warriors crossing the river. "Hold them, men!" he shouted as the warriors charged the hill. It was no use. The warriors broke through his line of men. The soldiers' frightened horses ran from the hilltop. Soon, the soldiers were surrounded by the enemy.

Native American warriors on horseback stormed through the groups of Custer's soldiers, firing their guns. The smaller groups of soldiers were easily killed. Many soldiers and warriors wrestled with one another on the ground. Custer fought with all of his strength alongside his men.

As far as Custer could see along the hill, soldiers in blue coats were fighting with bare-chested warriors. It seemed as if there were

three warriors to every soldier. It was then that Custer realized his mistake. His men were out-numbered. All Custer could do was fight and hope that Reno and Benteen were on their way from the south.

Dust and gun smoke thickened the air. Custer's eyes stung. Over the war cries and sounds of gunfire, he heard the rumbling of horses. More warriors were charging the hill. The soldiers fired their guns blindly at warriors they could hear but not see. The warriors attacked the hill with all their might.

In moments, the battle that came to be known as Custer's Last Stand was over. Custer's soldiers had fought fiercely, but they were no match for the thousands of warriors in the valley. As the smoke from the battle cleared, Custer and all 210 of his men lay dead.

Five miles away, Reno and Benteen had not been able to leave their hill. They did not know Custer and his men had all been killed. For them, the battle was not over.

25 Cents.

TRI

BISM

MASSACRED

GEN. CUSTER AND 261 MEN THE VICTIMS.

NO OFFICER OR MAN OF 5 COMPANIES LEFT TO TELL THE TALE.

3 Days Desperate Fighting by Maj. Reno and the Remainder of the Seventh.

Full Details of the Battle.

LIST OF KILLED AND WOUNDED

Bismarck Tribune's Special Correspondent Slain.

Squaws Mutilate and Rob Dead.

Victims Captured Alive. Tortured in Fiendish Manner.

What Will Congress Do About It

Shall This Be the Beginning of the End?

It will be remembered that the Bismarck Tribune sent a special correspondent with Gen. Terry, who was the only proffessional correspondent with the expedition. Kellogg's last words to the writer were: "We leave the Rosebud tomorrow and by the time this reaches you we will have

MET AND FOUGHT

hand conflict with a dozen or more Siouxs, emptying several chambers of his revolver, each time bringing a red-skin before he was brought down—shot thru the heart. It was here Bloody Knife surrendered his spirit to the one who gave it, fighting the natural and heriditary foes of his tribe, as well as the foes of the whites.

The Sioux dashed up beside the soldiers in some instances knocking them from their horses and killing them at their pleasure. This was the case with Lt. McIntosh, who was unarmed except with a saber. He was pulled from his horse, tortured and finally murdered at the pleasure of the red-devils. It was here that Fred Girard was separated from the command and lay all night with the screeching fiends dealing death and destruction to his comrades within a few feet of him, and, but time will not permit us to relate the story, through some means succeeded in saving his fine black stallion in which he took so much pride. The ford was crossed, the summit of the bluffs, having, Col. Smith says, the steepest sides that he ever saw ascended by a horse or mule reached, though the ascent was made under a galling fire.

Companies engaged in this affair were those of Captains Boylan, French and McIntosh. Col. Reno had gone ahead with these companies in obedience to the order of Gen. Custer, fighting most gallantly, driving back repeatedly the Indians who charged in their front, but the fire from the bluff being so galling, forced the movement heretofore alluded to. Signals were given and soon Benteen with the four companies in reserve came up in time to save

cept for the dead, Re brave men felt that nigh. Gen. Terry cam and strong men wept others necks, but no had from Custer. Ha and congratulations ly over when Lt. Br ed that he had found with one hundred an alry men. Imagin Words cannot pictu of these, his comr diers. Gen. Terry and found it to be those brave men Custer, all perished to tell the story o Those deployed as lay as they fell, sho every side, having surrounded in an ope men in companies toons, and like those mish line, lay as th their officers behind proper positions. who was shot throu and body, seemed to among the last to fall and near him lay th Col. Tom and Bosto ers, Col. Calhoun, hi law, and his nephew who insisted on accom expedition for pleasu and the members of t missioned staff a stripped of clothing of them with bodies tilated. The squaws passed over the field the skulls of the w dying with stones an heads of some were the body, the priva were cut off, while traces of torture, an been shot into their while yet or oth of te

This 1876 article from the *Bismarck Tribune* is an example of how one-sided the newspaper reports of the Battle of Little Bighorn were. The article tells the story as if Custer and his men were victims. It does not tell what happened from the Native American's point of view.

Chapter Five

THE FINAL FIGHT

After Reno, Benteen, and their men had made it to the hill, many warriors left them to fight Custer. Reno and Benteen had their men move all of the supplies and wounded soldiers into the center of the hill. The fighting slowed, but didn't stop. There was no way for them to get away without risking the lives of many men. Now that the battle with Custer was over, warriors who had left earlier returned to the hill to fight Reno once again. "They're coming at us from all sides, men! Hold strong!" Reno shouted. All around him, men quickly shot and reloaded their guns.

Reno hoped that the warriors would go back to their camps for the evening. Many of his men had been killed and many more were hurt. As the sun set, some warriors did leave, but the fight still did

not end. It lasted throughout the night and into the next day. Reno and Benteen's men fought with all their strength. Around 3:00 P.M., the warriors suddenly started to leave. As he looked out over the valley, Reno could see that the entire village was escaping. Reno and Benteen stayed on the hill and waited to see if the warriors were gone for good. They were puzzled. Had the warriors tired of fighting?

The Native Americans had left the valley because they had seen something that Reno and Benteen could not—a strong force of U.S. soldiers marching toward them. General Terry and Colonel Gibbon had finally made it to Little Bighorn.

Terry and Gibbon entered the valley as quickly as they could. On the way there, they received upsetting news from three of Custer's scouts who had escaped from the fighting. The men did not fully believe the horrors that the scouts spoke of until they arrived in the valley. What they saw was shocking. The bodies of hundreds of horses and men were scattered on the hills. Only one horse was left alive.

Eventually, the soldiers made it to the hill where Reno, Benteen, and their men were camped. There, they saw even more dead and wounded soldiers.

"General Terry! It is good to see you," Reno said. "Tell me, have you heard any news from Custer?"

Terry looked down at his hands and shook his head. "Custer is gone," he said. "His entire command was killed in the valley."

Reno's face grew pale. "We could not reach him, General," he said. "We have fought on this hill for the past two days. The fighting just ended this afternoon when the Indians must have seen you coming and left."

"Get your wounded men together. They will go back to Fort Lincoln," Terry said. "Everyone else will wait for more troops before moving on."

News of the battle at Little Bighorn spread quickly throughout the country. People were shocked that so many men were killed. They wanted the government to punish the Native Americans responsible for the deaths. Groups of soldiers called Custer's Avengers set out to find the Native Americans who were involved in the battle. Meanwhile, the Sioux and the Cheyenne Indians, who had joined together in the valley before the battle, were traveling and hunting buffalo for food. Soldiers found them and forced many to give up their freedom and live on reservations. In time, Native Americans across North America were forced to live on reservations. The Battle of Little Bighorn was their last major success.

General George Armstrong Custer was named a hero and buried at West Point, even though his last stand is thought of as the worst mistake in U.S. Army history. His last stand at the Battle of Little Bighorn will never be forgotten.

Glossary

career (kuh-RIHR) the work or the series of jobs that a person has, usually in the same profession

Gatling gun (GAT-ling GUN) a machine gun that can fire many bullets

lieutenant (loo-TEN-uhnt) an officer of low rank in the armed forces

military (MIL-uh-ter-ee) to do with soldiers, the armed forces, or war

reservation (rez-ur-VAY-shuhn) an area of land set aside by the government for a special purpose

retreat (ri-TREET) to move back or withdraw from a difficult situation

saddle (SAD-uhl) a leather seat for a rider on the back of a horse

tepees (TEE-peez) tents shaped like cones and made from animal skins by North American Indians

warrior (WOR-ee-ur) a soldier, or someone who is experienced in fighting battles

weapons (WEP-uhnz) things, such as swords, guns, knifes, or bombs, that can be used in a fight to attack or defend

Primary Sources

We can reconstruct the past by looking at important clues we find in things such as old photographs, drawings, and letters. We can use these items to help us draw conclusions about people and events in history. For instance, in Custer's last message on page 30, he orders Captain Benteen to come quick with men and bullets. He writes this upon discovering that the Native American village he's planning to attack is much larger than he thought. The message shows how bold Custer pushes forward, rather than call off the attack.

Primary sources can also be used to give us a better understanding of the time in which people of the past lived. The photograph on page 29 shows Custer, on horse, leading his troops and wagons through the Black Hills. We can compare and contrast the wagons and equipment they used then to the vehicles and equipment the military uses today. In these sources, we find the clues we need to solve the mysteries of the past.

In 1874 William H. Illingworth photographed Custer (left center in light clothing) leading his men through the Lakota land in the Black Hills. Two years later, Custer would meet his end at Little Bighorn.

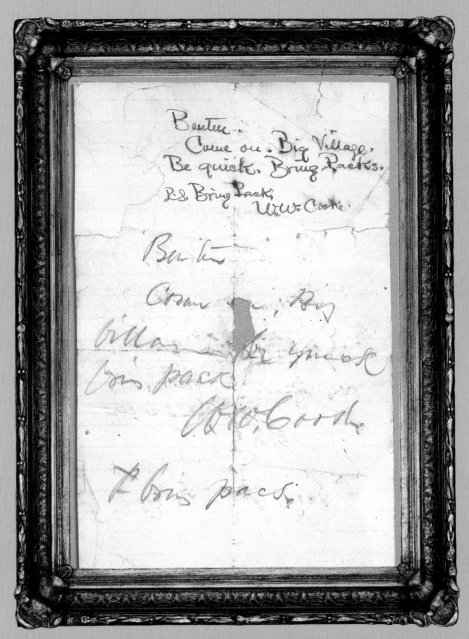

This note was Custer's last message to his troops. It reads, "Benteen—
Come on, Big village. Be quick, Bring packs." He was talking about
the bullets the pack mules were carrying.

Chief Kicking Bear fought at the Battle of Little Bighorn. He made this watercolor painting of the battle in 1898. Among the dead soldiers and Native Americans, we can see Custer in yellow buckskins and long hair on the left side of the painting.

This photo from 1909 shows Custer's Native American scouts visiting the spot where Custer was killed. The simple wooden cross marks where Custer died in battle.